Mom & Daughter Journal

By: Iona Yeung

Why journal?

These journal prompts are designed to strengthen the bond between a mother and daughter, to uncover things you may not know about each other before.

Because sometimes it's easier to put thoughts onto paper.
Take the time to reflect, ask questions, doodle, scribble.

To my daughter,
What I love about you...

_____

_____

_____

_____

_____

_____

_____

_____

_____

_____

_____

To my mom,
What I love about you...

_____

_____

_____

_____

_____

_____

_____

_____

_____

_____

_____

_____

To my daughter,
What is your idea of the perfect day?

_____

_____

_____

_____

_____

_____

_____

_____

_____

_____

_____

_____

To my mom,
What is your idea of the perfect day?

_____

_____

_____

_____

_____

_____

_____

_____

_____

_____

_____

_____

To my daughter,
When was the last time you felt really loved?

_____

_____

_____

_____

_____

_____

_____

_____

_____

_____

_____

_____

To my mom,
When was the last time you felt really loved?

_____

_____

_____

_____

_____

_____

_____

_____

_____

_____

_____

_____

To my daughter,
What's something you've always wanted to ask me?

_____

_____

_____

_____

_____

_____

_____

_____

_____

_____

_____

To my mom,
What's something you've always wanted to ask me?

_____

_____

_____

_____

_____

_____

_____

_____

_____

_____

_____

_____

To my daughter,
What's the scariest thing you've done?

_____

_____

_____

_____

_____

_____

_____

_____

_____

_____

_____

To my daughter,
What's the scariest thing you've done?

_____

_____

_____

_____

_____

_____

_____

_____

_____

_____

_____

To my daughter,
What's one thing you don't often tell your friends?

_____

_____

_____

_____

_____

_____

_____

_____

_____

_____

_____

_____

To my mom,
What's one thing you don't often tell your friends?

_____

_____

_____

_____

_____

_____

_____

_____

_____

_____

_____

_____

To my daughter,
If you could quite school/work and do whatever you want, what would you want to do?

_____

_____

_____

_____

_____

_____

_____

_____

_____

_____

_____

To my mom,
If you could quite school/work and do whatever you want, what would you want to do?

_____

_____

_____

_____

_____

_____

_____

_____

_____

_____

_____

_____

_____

To my daughter,
What do you admire in people your age?

_____

_____

_____

_____

_____

_____

_____

_____

_____

_____

_____

_____

To my mom,
What do you admire in people your age?

_____

_____

_____

_____

_____

_____

_____

_____

_____

_____

_____

_____

To my daughter,
What's something you'd like for us to do together?

_____

_____

_____

_____

_____

_____

_____

_____

_____

_____

_____

_____

To my mom,
What's something you'd like for us to do together?

_____

_____

_____

_____

_____

_____

_____

_____

_____

_____

_____

_____

To my daughter, what does your life look like in 5 years? Doodle it.

To my mom, what does your life look like in 5 years? Doodle it.

To my daughter,
What's one thing you've always wanted to tell me?

_____

_____

_____

_____

_____

_____

_____

_____

_____

_____

_____

_____

To my mom,
What's one thing you've always wanted to tell me?

_____

_____

_____

_____

_____

_____

_____

_____

_____

_____

_____

_____

To my daughter, do you see the glass full or empty?

Yes/No

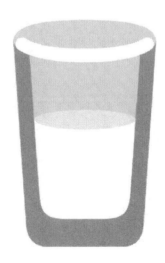

To my mom, do you see the glass full or empty?

Yes/No

To my daughter,
If you could eat one meal for the rest of your life, which would it be?

_____

_____

_____

_____

_____

_____

_____

_____

_____

_____

_____

To my mom,
If you could eat one meal for the rest of your life, which would it be?

_____

_____

_____

_____

_____

_____

_____

_____

_____

_____

_____

To my daughter,
Do you believe in love at first sight?

_____

_____

_____

_____

_____

_____

_____

_____

_____

_____

_____

_____

_____

To my mom,
Do you believe in love at first sight?

_____

_____

_____

_____

_____

_____

_____

_____

_____

_____

_____

_____

To my daughter,
If you were to learn something new, what would it be?

_____

_____

_____

_____

_____

_____

_____

_____

_____

_____

To my mom,
If you were to learn something new, what would it be?

_____

_____

_____

_____

_____

_____

_____

_____

_____

_____

_____

_____

To my daughter,
Do you have a secret talent?

_____

_____

_____

_____

_____

_____

_____

_____

_____

_____

_____

_____

_____

To my mom,
Do you have a secret talent?

_____

_____

_____

_____

_____

_____

_____

_____

_____

_____

_____

_____

_____

_____

To my daughter,
If the world were to end tomorrow, what would you do today?

_____

_____

_____

_____

_____

_____

_____

_____

_____

_____

_____

_____

To my mom,
If the world were to end tomorrow, what would you do today?

_____

_____

_____

_____

_____

_____

_____

_____

_____

_____

_____

_____

To my daughter,
What's one song you can listen to over and over again?

_____

_____

_____

_____

_____

_____

_____

_____

_____

_____

_____

To my mom,
What's one song you can listen to over and over again?

_____

_____

_____

_____

_____

_____

_____

_____

_____

_____

_____

_____

To my daughter,
What's one movie you can watch over and over again?

_____

_____

_____

_____

_____

_____

_____

_____

_____

_____

_____

To my mom,
What's one movie you can watch over and over again?

_____

_____

_____

_____

_____

_____

_____

_____

_____

_____

_____

_____

To my daughter,
If you could be a super hero for the day,
which one would you be?

_____

_____

_____

_____

_____

_____

_____

_____

_____

_____

_____

_____

To my mom,
If you could be a super hero for the day,
which one would you be?

_____

_____

_____

_____

_____

_____

_____

_____

_____

_____

_____

To my daughter,
What's something that makes you sad?

_____

_____

_____

_____

_____

_____

_____

_____

_____

_____

_____

To my mom,
What's something that makes you sad?

_____

_____

_____

_____

_____

_____

_____

_____

_____

_____

_____

_____

_____

To my daughter,
What's something that always makes you happy?

_____

_____

_____

_____

_____

_____

_____

_____

_____

_____

To my mom,
What's something that always makes you happy?

_____

_____

_____

_____

_____

_____

_____

_____

_____

_____

_____

_____

_____

To my daughter,
What's something that always makes you sad?

_____

_____

_____

_____

_____

_____

_____

_____

_____

_____

_____

_____

To my mom,
What's something that always makes you sad?

_____

_____

_____

_____

_____

_____

_____

_____

_____

_____

_____

_____

_____

To my daughter,
What should I do to cheer you up when you're sad?

_____

_____

_____

_____

_____

_____

_____

_____

_____

_____

_____

_____

To my mom,
What should I do to cheer you up when you're sad?

_____

_____

_____

_____

_____

_____

_____

_____

_____

_____

_____

_____

To my daughter,
What's one thing you enjoy doing together?

_____

_____

_____

_____

_____

_____

_____

_____

_____

_____

_____

To my mom,
What's one thing you enjoy doing together?

_____

_____

_____

_____

_____

_____

_____

_____

_____

_____

_____

_____

To my daughter,
What's on your bucket list?

_____

_____

_____

_____

_____

_____

_____

_____

_____

_____

_____

_____

_____

To my mom,
What's on your bucket list?

_____

_____

_____

_____

_____

_____

_____

_____

_____

_____

_____

_____

_____

_____

To my daughter,
What can I do to get to know you better?

_____

_____

_____

_____

_____

_____

_____

_____

_____

_____

_____

_____

To my mom,
What can I do to get to know you better?

_____

_____

_____

_____

_____

_____

_____

_____

_____

_____

_____

_____

_____

_____

To my daughter, let's play a game

Let's play again

Best 2 out of 3?

To my daughter, this is what my perfect day looks like in drawing...

To my mom, this is what my perfect day looks like in drawing...

Things for us to share

Our joint bucket list

_____

_____

_____

_____

_____

_____

_____

_____

_____

_____

_____

_____

_____

A list of movies we can watch together

A list of books we can read and discuss

_____

_____

_____

_____

_____

_____

_____

_____

_____

_____

_____

_____

Things to do together this year

_____

_____

_____

_____

_____

_____

_____

_____

_____

_____

_____

_____

_____

Letters

One for every month of the year

Letters to my daughter

Letters to my daughter

_____

_____

_____

_____

_____

_____

_____

_____

_____

_____

_____

_____

Letters to my daughter

Letters to my daughter

_____

_____

_____

_____

_____

_____

_____

_____

_____

_____

_____

_____

_____

Letters to my daughter

Letters to my daughter

Letters to my daughter

Letters to my daughter

_____

_____

_____

_____

_____

_____

_____

_____

_____

_____

_____

_____

_____

Letters to my daughter

_____

_____

_____

_____

_____

_____

_____

_____

_____

_____

_____

_____

_____

Letters to my daughter

Letters to my daughter

Letters to my daughter

Letters to my mom

Letters to my mom

Letters to my mom

Letters to my mom

Letters to my mom

_____

_____

_____

_____

_____

_____

_____

_____

_____

_____

_____

_____

_____

_____

_____

Letters to my mom

_____

_____

_____

_____

_____

_____

_____

_____

_____

_____

_____

_____

Letters to my mom

Letters to my mom

Letters to my mom

Letters to my mom

Notes & Doodles

Use this to unleash your creativity

Made in the USA
San Bernardino, CA
14 May 2019